BUILDING A PLACE FOR US

DAVID GOODE-CROSS, PHD

BUILDING A PLACE FOR US

HOW TO CREATE A SOLO PRIVATE PRACTICE TO SERVE BLACK CLIENTS

The Goode Doctor LLC

Like many of you, I've been blessed by the Creator with family and friends who loved me into being the person I am. The number of people who have supported and encouraged me along the way is far too long to list, but I dedicate this book to two amazing Black women psychologists who were instrumental in my development:

To A.M.W., who first told me that I was more than enough but never too much. Thank you for affirming me and for teaching me to affirm myself.

To W.C.M., who exemplified Black excellence and radical authenticity. Thank you for teaching me all that I know and reminding me of all that I am.

CONTENTS

Acknowledgments
iv

Introduction
1

1 — Am I ready to go out on my own?
3

2 — Do I have the necessary skills to run a practice?
6

3 — Can I make the money I want in private practice?
8

4 — Can I deal with the stresses of practice ownership?
13

5 — How do I develop and refine the purpose, vision, and goals for my practice?
15

6 — Whom do I intend to serve and why?
19

7 — How do I name my practice?
23

8 — How much money does it take to start a practice?
27

9 — How much should I charge for my services?
32

10 — What happens if I decide to take insurance?
36

11 — How much should I spend on renting an office?
39

CONTENTS

12 — How much should I spend to furnish my office?
43

13 — How do I select a health records system?
48

14 — How do I manage the finances in a private practice?
50

15 — How do I effectively market the practice?
53

16 — What kind of support will I need?
57

Conclusion
61

About The Author
62

INTRODUCTION

Just like some of you reading this, I was trained as a counseling psychologist. I came to Baltimore in 2011 for a new faculty job at a therapist training graduate program in the area. I had always sworn to myself that I, unlike most of my own professors in graduate school, would continue to practice as a therapist while I was teaching. Shortly after getting licensed as a psychologist in Maryland, I set out to establish a boutique practice aimed at Black and LGBTQ+ folks. My entire graduate training had been focused on the unique needs of these clients, and I'd even written a few research articles on the subject that were published in reputable journals. I figured that with my expertise, I'd have no problem building a client base.

I could not have been more wrong. I won't bore you with all the mistakes that I made, but suffice it to say that I lost money on the practice for the next three years until I shut it down. In the years since I relaunched (and eventually expanded) the practice, I learned many lessons about how to build and grow a successful private practice. I wrote this book to share with all you the hard-learned lessons in running a business so that you can avoid making them.

I was not taught anything about the business of practice in graduate school, and I had to adapt what I learned to working with Black populations through my own research, coaching, and trial and error. In the pages that follow, I aim to help Black therapists who aspire to run private practices that will ultimately serve their (and our) communities. My wish for any reader is to have an abundant, joy-filled life of service that allows you to make a good living doing the work you feel passionate about. This book is my attempt to help you with that.

Now let's get started.

AM I READY TO GO OUT ON MY OWN?

It depends.

The fantasy of practicing independently is appealing to clinicians new and old. However, the reality of being your own boss brings many unforeseen challenges that are often ignored by therapists who are looking to make the leap into practice. Creating a solo practice requires skills in running a business that can be learned easily. Ultimately, however, launching out on your own requires a great deal of risk tolerance.

On the clinical side, you need to be able to make ethical decisions independently and be prepared to justify your actions to clients, their families, insurance companies, and perhaps a court of law. On the business side, you'll also need to manage the ups and downs of income and the added responsibility of leases and other agreements that ensure your practice can exist. Your ability to function without the safety net of an agency and hold all of the stresses that come with the sometimes-life-and-death nature of our work is critical. In short, if you have ample coping strategies to manage the anxieties concomitant with the choice to open a practice, you're ready to go out on your own.

For new and/or provisionally licensed therapists: You're defi-nitely not.

It's a terrible idea for provisionally licensed therapists to work in solo practice.

Because of the shortage of mental health professionals, some insurance panels will credential provisionally licensed therapists as long as they have an identified supervisor. This flies in the face of the collective wisdom of state licensing boards that dictate a period of supervised practice before therapists can gain their independent license as a counselor, marriage and family therapist, psychologist, or social worker.

Most therapist training programs are woefully light on stressing the importance of theories of psychotherapy and facilitating change. Most clinicians, regardless of their discipline, have taken 1-2 survey courses covering hundreds of theories in 12-15 weeks. As a result, most graduates have acquired only a vague understanding of what supposedly works in therapy, along with a toolbox of disparate interventions cobbled together from what they have read, learned from supervisors, and what they innately believe about the change process. Novice (and sometimes experienced) clinicians don't know what they don't know, and they can feel prematurely prepared to "hang out their shingle."

I strongly discourage new graduates from starting their private practices at least until they have completed their supervised experience. They may need to delay launching their practices further if they did not receive high-quality supervision.

Being in a solo private practice means that you hold ultimate clinical and legal responsibility for your work as a therapist. Unlike being in an agency, school, or medical setting, the buck stops with you. After-hours and crisis calls are your responsibility. The decision to hospitalize or report abuse and neglect is yours alone. If you are an in-network provider for insurance companies, you may be expected to be available 24/7 for client emergencies. The responsibilities are grave for a private practitioner and must be carefully considered before beginning a solo practice.

DO I HAVE THE NECESSARY SKILLS TO RUN A PRACTICE?

Maybe. But even if you don't, you can hire some help.

Successfully running a practice takes a measure of organizational skill. In addition to adhering to the legal and ethical standards for client documentation, practice owners are subject to insurance payer regulations around the provision of clinical practice. If you've worked at another agency that was a HIPAA-covered entity, much of this will be familiar to you.

You'll also need to manage the business side of the practice. Every practice owner must track all business receipts and ensure that expenses stay within the budget they've developed for the financial health of the practice. Billing for cash-pay practices is typically straightforward, but billing for insurance-based practices is more complex. Practice owners must stay on top of insurance claims to make sure they are submitted in time for reimbursement. They'll also need to track accounts receivable, outstanding balances from clients and insurance companies, to ensure they are paid for the services that they render.

Before going into private practice, you should ask yourself if you:

1. have the kinds of organizational skills that will allow you to run your practice effectively and/or
2. are willing to pay for administrative, accounting, or billing support if you do not.

I have seen incredibly gifted therapists falter because they did not have the support that they needed to manage the business side of their practices.

CAN I MAKE THE MONEY I WANT IN PRIVATE PRACTICE?

Probably.

I'll try to break down the math you'll need to determine whether you can attain what you want in the following example.

Daniel is a licensed psychologist. For the past several years, he's had a small private practice to generate extra income in addition to his day job at a local college counseling center. During that time, Daniel's average revenue per session has been about $125. His goal is to make $100,000 annually before taxes. Assuming Daniel gives himself four weeks off for vacation, holiday, and sick time, he would be working 48 weeks per year. Thus, our first formula is calculating Daniel's desired weekly salary:

$100,000 / 48 weeks = $2083.33 per week

This is where it gets tricky. The $2083.33 is a *gross* figure. To earn $100,000 pretax, Daniel must account for his expenses such as rent, internet services, software, etc.—which we will estimate as about 35% of his gross. (We will cover expenses in a later section.) Thus, to figure out how many sessions Daniel needs to do, we must do more math. This may be the one and only time your high school algebra comes in handy.

First, we have to determine what Daniel must gross in order to net $2083.33:

$2083.33 = 65% of Daniel's gross weekly income, or
$2088.33 = .65x
$2083.33 / .65 = x
$3205.12 = x,

Daniel must gross **$3205.12** each week to generate a weekly salary of $2083.33. Now we translate that into sessions. If Daniel's revenue averages $125 per session, then we can calculate the number of sessions he needs by dividing the gross revenue by the number of sessions, or

$3205.12 / 125 = 25.64 or roughly 26 sessions per week.

That's in a perfect world, but we all know no such place exists. Among psychotherapists, a 10% no-show/cancellation rate is typical. Daniel should factor that in and over-schedule to ensure his productivity goal gets met:

.90x = 26 clients
x = 26 / .9
x = 28.888

Daniel will need to schedule about 29 client hours each week to ensure he achieves his income goals.

The number of clients Daniel needs to see each week is directly proportional to the average revenue he earns per session. But let's say that Daniel's average revenue per session is $100. Then he'd need to see between 32 and 33 clients each week to make that same money (using the formulas stated above). Conversely, Daniel may decide to give himself six weeks off per year instead of four; he'd need to see 27 clients each week and schedule 30. All those numbers directly affect how much he'd need to work and charge for his sessions.

Once you calculate the number of sessions necessary to make your desired income, you'll have crucial information to help you determine how feasible your income goals are and if they align with your own capacity for client work.

All things being equal, if you're a therapist in private practice with a continually full caseload, you will likely make more money than you would working in a group practice or at an agency. You will probably also have greater control over your schedule, and you can craft your caseload to align more with your areas of clinical expertise and interest. But here's the rub: That additional money comes at a cost—time that is uncompensated.

When you work for an agency or group practice, the organization will probably manage administrative and marketing tasks like recruiting clients, billing, answering phone calls and emails, and other behind-the-scenes tasks that help you get and keep clients. You will get paid an hourly wage or a percentage split (usually between 40-55%), and you'll get paid as an employee (or as a contractor).

To return to Daniel, let's calculate how much he actually earns for the work he puts in. Daniel spends about three hours weekly on documentation and another 12 hours responding to clients and inquiries, managing insurance payments and/or billing, keeping the office clean and well stocked, and completing the small tasks that keep his business functional. In actuality, he is working about 40 hours a week, so his hourly wage is:

$2083.33 / 40 hours, or $52.08

Let's imagine that Daniel's twin sister, Danielle, is also a psychologist working at a group practice down the street. Her sessions also command $125 per hour, and Danielle negotiated a 50% split with the practice owners. Her hourly wage is $62.50 for each clinical hour. She also spends three hours each week completing her documentation, which is uncompensated. Assuming she also sees 26 clients per week, Danielle's income is:

$62.50 x 26 hours, or $1625

Even though Danielle takes home less money than her twin brother, her hourly wage is actually higher. Because she only works 29 hours, her hourly wage is:

$1625 / 29 hours, or $56.03

Although almost $4 looks like a small difference in hourly wages, it's much larger when you factor in paying self-employment taxes of about 15% as a practice owner versus FICA taxes at about 7.65% as an employee. (Discussing tax liabilities is beyond the scope of this book, so you should consult a tax or accounting professional for a more detailed explanation.) The point of this illustration is that even though Daniel makes more money for seeing the same number of clients, he works over ⅓ more hours than Danielle to earn it!

To restate, as a clinician in private practice you will likely make more money than by working for someone else. But if you work for someone else, you will have more time for other activities or to see more clients if you want to make more money. My point is not to dissuade you from starting your own practice, but I want to be clear that you'll be working much harder for that higher salary you'll earn as a practice owner. You must decide if that extra effort is worth it to you. Plus, there are other risks associated with a private practice that I'll discuss in the next section.

CAN I DEAL WITH THE STRESSES OF PRACTICE OWNERSHIP?

In terms of businesses, running a private practice is a fairly straightforward model: You get a professional license, you rent and decorate a space (or not), you recruit clients, you see those clients, and you collect money from the clients and/or an insurance company on behalf of those clients. It's simple, but it's not necessarily easy. There is risk involved with any entrepreneurial endeavor. In the case of a private practice, the biggest risk involves timing and money.

Unless you're planning to establish an all cash-pay practice, there will always be a lull between when you render services and when you get paid. I'll discuss the advantages and disadvantages of accepting insurance in your practice later, but the vast number of private practices—particularly those who serve primarily Black clients—accept insurance. Accepting insurance generally expands the number of clients who can access your services. In exchange, you'll need to wait to be reimbursed for the services you render. This time can be between 1-2 weeks or 1-3 months, depending on the laws in your state, the efficiency of the insurance carriers' claims processing, and the whims of the postal service. Additionally, insurance-based practices are subject to the occasional insurance payment errors, audits, and clawbacks.

Beyond the perils of dealing with insurance payers, there tends to be a natural ebb and flow of clients. In the summer, existing clients may take vacations and new client referrals often slow. In the fall and winter (particularly around the holidays), client referrals generally increase. As a result, your practice income will wax and wane. Furthermore, some clinicians have a harder time getting full than others. Because there are relatively few Black therapists, this isn't usually a problem in locations with lots of Black folks. But in rural areas where Black clients are few, or if you have an obscure specialty, you may have some periods when you are less full than you'd like. Practice owners have to manage their income accordingly or at the very least manage their expectations around making money.

Steady paychecks aren't guaranteed in private practice. You must honestly ask yourself if you have the nerves to manage the ups and downs of your income. It's a gamble. The risks are relatively low, but they aren't zero. My experience is that most therapists tend towards anxiety, so this kind of uncertainty will likely cause distress on a not-infrequent basis. If you're one of the small minority of Americans who has a sizable savings and an emergency account—or if you have a family situation that provides you similar security—you're in good shape. If you're not, being an entrepreneur will require you to get comfortable with knowing that financial ruin (or at least discomfort) is an omnipresent threat.

HOW DO I DEVELOP AND REFINE THE PURPOSE, VISION, AND GOALS FOR MY PRACTICE?

As therapists in the age of managed care, most of us understand the importance of developing treatment plans and goals for our client work. Yet, we may have trouble operationalizing the amorphous desires we have for our private practice. In this section, I offer some guidance to help you differentiate between your personal, clinical, and financial objectives for your practice.

PURPOSE

Lest you spend unnecessary time trying to sort out your purpose, I'll tell you what it is: *to make a profit*. Period. Unless you aim to create a structure that receives external funding in perpetuity, the only purpose of your practice is to ensure its own viability. Your practice must eke out enough money after deducting taxes and expenses to support your life. Although it is a simple truth, fulfilling this purpose can sometimes be difficult.

VISION

If the purpose of your practice reflects the realities of being a business owner, the vision of your practice is based on your personal and professional values. The vision reflects your pie-in-the-sky hopes and aspirations for what your practice will become. Many people create vision boards or other tangible expressions of their deepest desires. Your vision statement would articulate something about the services you wish to provide, who you wish to serve, and how you wish to be perceived. I have included the vision statement for my group practice, East Towson Psychological Services, as an example:

> *East Towson Psychological Services will be the premier practice for nurturing therapists who wish to deepen their expertise in working with clients of color, and gender and sexual minorities. We will provide culturally and clinically responsive care to clients and offer services to expand the knowledge of therapists in the community.*

Like the U.S. Constitution, your vision statement serves both as an aspirational document and a proclamation of how your practice will function. It may be useful to engage in some exercises to help you clarify your personal and professional values before creating your vision statement.

GOALS

There are as many goals as there are clinicians and practices. For some therapists, the goal of opening a private practice may be to make more money than would be possible from working in other settings. Others may be interested in curating a specific client population or specializing in a particular modality of treatment. Still others may be interested in the flexibility and lifestyle that being in private practice can offer. Whether your reasons for wanting to open a practice are listed above or are completely different, the structure of your business will be determined, at least in part, by the goals you set for the practice.

To illustrate, if your goal for practice is to make as much money as possible, you would need to consider whether it was financially feasible to join one or more insurance panels where the reimbursement rates are determined by the insurer rather than having a strictly cash-pay (also called fee-for-service) practice in which clients pay the fees that you set. Conversely, if your goal is to help as many children as possible, you may need to consider getting empaneled with the Medicaid program in your state, since Medicaid is the largest insurer of children in the U.S. If you wanted flexibility to take care of your children or other loved ones, you would build a practice very differently than if your primary goal were to work with school-aged children and adolescents.

You should spend time pondering your specific hopes, dreams, and goals for your practice. Some questions to consider include:

- Why am I considering private practice as a potential work setting?
- What are the demographic markers of the clients I wish to see?
- What are my specific income goals for working in or starting a private practice?
- How many hours per week am I willing to see clients? How many hours per day?
- What are my time constraints and preferences for therapy hours?
- How much interaction with colleagues do I require for optimal support? For clinical consultation?

This list is not exhaustive, but it can help you begin to clarify your goals for opening and working in a private practice. Most therapists have a vague idea of the answers to some of these questions, but they may not have thought through the implications of the answers. Here's what I mean. Let's say that you want to work with BIPOC kids, but you don't want to deal with the challenges of navigating insurance reimbursements. The decision not to take Medicaid or commercial insurance limits your potential pool of clients to the children of parents who can either afford to pay your fees (i.e., wealthy parents) or to parents with great out-of-network benefits and disposable income that would enable them to wait for insurance reimbursement. Because of the lingering effects of systemic racism and current inequality, this pool of potential clients will likely not include a great number of Black, Latinx or Indigenous children. By deciding against taking insurance, you would essentially be committing yourself to working with affluent and most likely White children. This part would not align with your stated goal of working with BIPOC kids and would likely lead to dissatisfaction. To use a different example, you might choose to keep "banker's hours"—seeing clients between 10am and 3pm. This might be great if you work with preschoolers, but it might be more challenging if you intend to draw working folks who will be at their jobs while you are available.

Having a clear understanding of your purpose, vision, and goals will inform how you build your business. Your job is to create all three and find the points of convergence, as well as to work through the potential ways that your mission, vision, and goal may be in conflict. Once you establish what the vision and goals are for your practice, you'll be able to make other decisions that support them and your purpose. And, if you see that some of your choices are out of alignment with your desires, you can either revise your vision and goals or make different decisions.

WHOM DO I INTEND TO SERVE AND WHY?

Therapists will often identify reasons for entering the profession, such as their own or their family's history of psychological distress, a desire to improve their own mental health and wellbeing, and the desire to decrease suffering. Our work most often has deeply personal roots, whether we care to admit it or not. Clinical supervision and consultation can help practitioners examine their own motives for working with their intended client population.

From a business perspective, it is important to remember that even if you see your work as a calling or an opportunity to work through your own unresolved issues, the ultimate purpose of your practice is to be profitable. Keeping that in mind will help ensure that your best intentions and purity of spirit don't lead you to build a practice that loses money. None of your potential clients can be served if your business is not financially viable.

Whom you intend to serve will greatly affect how your business will take shape. Below, I share some of the business considerations I pondered when forming my own practice, East Towson Psychological Services:

- **Whom we serve**: Black and other clients of color, LGBTQ+ clients
- **Location**: Just north of a major, predominantly Black city (Baltimore, Md.), just off the exit of a major highway
- **Name**: East Towson Psychological Services—East Towson is an historic community of emancipated persons in Baltimore County
- **Finances**: We accept insurance reimbursement. Because of the ongoing and pernicious effects of systemic racism, many Black clients, even those considered middle class, struggle to pay out-of-pocket for therapy. Hence, to ensure most of our clients are Black, we are empaneled with some insurance payers.
- **Hours**: Because most of our clients work, therapists in our practice are required to work at least two evenings and one weekend day.

Additionally, here are some of the clinical factors that affect our work with clients:

- **Issues of discrimination-related and/or relational trauma**: Most of our clients have at least one marginalized identity, and many have more than one. Our clinical work, therefore, also involves treating the negative consequences of racist, heterosexist, and cis-normative microaggressions. Workplace discrimination and family of origin concerns are often other areas of focus.
- **Transition-related care**: Some of our clients desire to begin or continue gender-affirming medical care. Many insurance carriers require a psychological assessment prior to approving such treatment, which we provide.
- **Romantic relationship therapy**: Most Black therapists in our region offer faith-based therapy (i.e., Christian coun-

seling). Very few Black and Brown therapists have comfort and expertise in treating same-sex couples or partners in polyamorous relationships. We offer this service to fill a community need.

· **Training**: We offer a robust training program because very few therapists know much about the intricacies of working with QTPOC populations. This training involves external supervision, monthly training seminars by local and national experts, and numerous other supervision and learning opportunities.

A critical step early in the process of developing your practice is to develop a client avatar. You want to think through who the ideal client is for your practice, including sociodemographic characteristics, presenting concerns, treatment preferences, and pain points. What does your ideal client want or need? Although this may seem like a silly exercise, it will help you greatly when it comes to marketing, which we will discuss in a later chapter, as well as considering the services you plan to offer.

Every clinician in our practice creates a client avatar. One therapist named their avatar "Keith" who was described as a 35-year-old, gay/queer-identified, Black, cis-male. Keith's current socioeconomic position is middle class, and he struggles with imposter syndrome and over-functioning. Keith has dating issues because he's a little emotionally unavailable due to his interpersonal guardedness.

Keith's Presenting concerns:

Anxiety, depression, mood disorders, stress, dissociation, maladaptive coping mechanisms, chronic illnesses, cognitive distortions, identity development struggles

Keith's Pain points:

Shame, invisibility, feeling unheard, misunderstood, withdrawn, overworked/spread thin, self-hatred, numbness, feeling undeserving, unworthiness

Our practice deliberately fills a small but critical niche in our community—Black clients of all sexualities and genders. Your practice may not have such a targeted ideal client population. Whether or not your desired niche is as small as ours, it's important to remember that whom you serve will dictate how you serve.

HOW DO I NAME MY PRACTICE?

Historically, Black folks have used names to creatively pay homage to our heritage and embody our cultures. In the context of naming a child, such creativity can be empowering. When naming a business, however, some choices may hinder present and future growth. Naming your business should be a measured, rational decision rather than one based solely on emotion or personal preference. Below, I offer suggestions to help you create a name for your practice that supports your purpose (i.e., profitability) and vision.

DON'T USE YOUR NAME!

I am 100% sure that your parents picked a wonderful name for you. They probably were not intending for it to be the name of a business, so you shouldn't either. Regardless of how elegant, regal, of pretty your name is, using it as your business name limits you. If you ever plan to retire or sell your practice, your name will not be valuable to a potential buyer. And even if it were, you wouldn't want someone else to have access to it. Also, should you decide to form a group practice, an eponymously named practice will make recruiting clients for the other therapists in the practice challenging. Think about it: If you found Dana Smith Counseling online, would you choose to see Karen Jones or Dana Smith? Right. That's what everyone else is thinking. You may think that you'll never want to sell your practice or form a group, but it's just as easy to *not* name the practice after yourself as to give the future you more options.

LOCATION-BASED NAMES

Practices such as the Therapy Group of D.C. or East Towson Psychological Services are named, in part, after where they are. Generally, a word to denote the services offered (e.g., counseling, therapy, psychology, etc.) is added to the neighborhood or locality. Some advantages of such names are their ease of searchability and that they help potential clients quickly locate services in their area. Practices named after locations may also be easier to sell. Potential drawbacks can include locking the practice into a specific location and possible confusion if there are several practices with similar names in an area (e.g., Therapy Center of Cleveland and The Cleveland Family Therapy Center).

SPECIALTY-BASED NAMES

Some practices embed their specialties in their names. The names may be based on a particular specialized client population (e.g., Woman's Growth Center), a specific disorder or presenting concern (e.g., Anxiety Treatment Center), or a particular modality of treatment (e.g., DBT Treatment of Atlanta). Often, locations are combined with a particular specialty to create the name of the practice. One advantage to these names that denote the practice specialty is that potential clients can quickly identify if they want such specialized care. A potential disadvantage includes clients' disinterest or uncertainty if they are well suited for the practice specialty. For example, can a cis-man be seen at the Women's Growth Center? Can someone at the Anxiety Treatment Center treat clients' anxiety as well as their depression? Can a trans person get help at Columbia Christian Counseling? Practices with these sorts of names are also easier to sell to a potential buyer if you decide to sell the business.

SYMBOLIC NAMES

Black therapists and other BIPOC therapists may use symbols or imagery to name their practices. Adinkra or Ancient Egyptian/Kemetian symbols may inspire some names like Aya Psychology or Sankofa Psychotherapy. Such names may have the advantage of informing clients who have prior knowledge of these symbols of the practice's values or beliefs. They may make logo design easier, should owners choose to use the symbol. A disadvantage is that such symbols are commonly used so it may be difficult to establish any real brand equity with one in your design.

OUTCOME-BASED NAMES

Naming a practice based on the expected or promised outcome is another often-used strategy. The Wellness Center, Mental Wellness Counseling, or Turning Point Counseling are examples of outcome-based names. The purpose of these names is simply to signal what clients may expect as a result of engaging in these services. These sorts of names may potentially be catchy and attract some clients, although they may also not provide enough specificity about the type of treatment provided to potential clients.

The aforementioned categories are but a sampling of the conventions used to name private practices. Perhaps what's most important is the intention behind the name you choose. Your practice name should reflect your values and skills while appealing to your dream clients. For example, Aya Psychology may reflect your value of African-centered thought while also appealing to Black clients who understand that symbolism. One mistake Black therapists can make is naming their practice to appeal to a very broad audience but still only attracting a limited client population. The unvarnished truth is that stereotypes of Black people's intelligence and competence continue to abound; the potential clients for Black therapists (and all BIPOC therapists) are automatically limited. Therefore, I recommend against trying to appeal only or primarily to White clients as this strategy will likely backfire.

HOW MUCH MONEY DOES IT TAKE TO START A PRACTICE?

There's good and bad news about the costs associated with starting a private practice. The good news is that, unlike many other health and wellness-related small businesses, the upfront costs are relatively low. The bad news, however, is that the costs aren't $0. If money is already a challenge, you may struggle to find the extra cash to start your business. Start-up costs range from $1000 to $5000, with the bulk of the cost being associated with office rental. Obviously, location is an important variable, as rents can vary greatly.

I've broken the start-up costs into four general categories:

1. foundational business expenses
2. acquiring and furnishing office space
3. computer equipment and software expenses
4. insurance coverages

I'll provide a brief overview of each type of expense and the rationale for it, but this information isn't a substitute for legal, accounting, or other professional advice.

FOUNDATIONAL BUSINESS EXPENSES

Though you are the heart, soul, and workhorse of your practice, it still must be a separate entity from you. Below are listed some essential steps to establish your practice as an official business and an estimate of their costs:

1. Obtain a federal employer identification number (EIN). The EIN is like a social security number for businesses; you get one through the IRS website for free.
2. Establish a state business structure. Most practice owners establish their practice as some sort of corporation—most often an LLC or PLLC. This is done through the business agency or department of commerce in your state. It's cheaper to do it yourself, but it's probably better to use an attorney or company (e.g., LegalZoom, etc.) to establish it. The cost can range from a couple hundred dollars to about $2500 depending on which method you use.
3. Acquire a national provider identifier (NPI) number. If you have been providing billable services, you already have this number. If not, you can obtain one through the Centers for Medicare & Medicaid Services (CMS) online, and it's free.
4. Open business checking accounts. You should establish at least three checking accounts (I'll explain why later) with a bank using your EIN. The minimum opening balance can vary but will likely be about $500 for each account.

Additionally, therapists who choose to get empaneled with insurance companies may pay someone to help them get credentialed. These fees can range between $150-$300 per insurance panel, depending on region.

OFFICE SPACE

Although telehealth has gained popularity due to the COVID-19 pandemic, most clinicians will still need a physical office space. Insurance companies require a physical address for credentialing. Unless you plan on having an exclusively cash-pay practice doing telehealth, finding an office location is an important part of establishing your business. Depending on the space, there will likely be other associated expenses. (Therapists may be tempted to use their home address and run a virtual or in-person practice from there. I advise against this for privacy and safety reasons.) Here are some of the types of expenses related to procuring suitable office space:

1. Lease or sublease: Your office rental expenses will be determined by the hours you'll be open and the primary medium through which you will operate—full, part time, face to face, and/or telehealth. If you intend to work part-time and/or primarily via telehealth, subletting will likely be the most cost-effective way to start your practice. Subletting arrangements may vary from a flat hourly or daily rate to a percentage per client seen. Sublease terms are typically also shorter in comparison to having one's own lease, which are frequently 3-5 years. Whether you decide to lease or sublet, your rental expenses should be no more than 10% of your projected income generated from the space. We will explore this in greater detail in a subsequent chapter.

2. Furnishings: Plan to spend no more than $2000 to furnish your office. I'll expand on this in a later part of this book.

COMPUTER EQUIPMENT AND SOFTWARE

Thankfully, the days of paper charts are long gone. Thus, you'll need to ensure that your technology can meet the needs of your practice. At a minimum, you'll need:

1. Laptop/tablet
2. Wi-Fi/Internet access
3. Printer
4. Scanner (or scanning app for another device)
5. Mobile phone or HIPAA-compliant communication system
6. Electronic health record (EHR)
7. Website (domain, development, and hosting)
8. Credit card/point-of-sale terminal
9. Secure email

INSURANCE COVERAGES

As a practice owner, you'll need two types of insurance—professional and personal—but the types of insurance will vary according to your individual situation. At a minimum, you will need professional liability insurance, which you likely already have. Additionally, most property managers will require lessors to have renter's insurance, often called "slip and fall" coverage as a condition of the lease. As a sublessor you may be covered under the primary tenant's policy, so double check. Verify with your state if need worker's compensation coverage.

Personnel policies are completely dependent on the individual needs of the practice owner. Health, dental, and vision insurance, as well as short- and long-term disability and term-life insurance may be necessary. Your decision to work with an insurance broker to acquire this coverage will depend on whether you can obtain these policies through another employer (yours or your partner's) or a healthcare exchange.

There is no reason to incur all these expenses at once, unless you choose to. For therapists with limited disposable income, working to acquire the equipment and business structure can happen over time, which allows you to spread out the expense. Some practice owners take the plunge and use credit cards or borrow against other assets (like retirement accounts) or from loved ones to fund their practice. So long as you choose frugally, your business should be able to recoup the initial investment within a year of opening your practice.

HOW MUCH SHOULD I CHARGE FOR MY SERVICES?

Most therapists make the mistake of setting their fees randomly. They look online to see what other therapists in their area are charging, then set their fees higher or lower based on how they feel about themselves in relation to those numbers. If it's not obvious, that isn't a particularly useful strategy for determining your livelihood. There are a few schools of thought related to setting your client fees, but I'll discuss two in this section. Both are methods based on calculations, but the data on which the calculations are based differ.

METHOD 1: FAIR MARKET VALUE

The first data-driven way of determining your fees is by exploring existing consumer data for your area. Databases such as the FAIR Health (https://www.fairhealthconsumer.org) can provide an estimate of in-network and out-of-network costs for CPT codes associated with psychotherapy.

For example, my practice is in the ZIP code 21286. The CPT code for Psychotherapy, 60 minutes is 90837. According to the FAIR Health consumer database:

In-network price: $111

Private pay/Out-of-network price: $175

The caveat to this method is that most databases aggregate what insurance carriers pay for a particular CPT code or service without regard to the credentials of the provider. Using the example above, the figures listed are average reimbursement cost and out-of-network costs for all mental health providers—including counselors, psychiatrists, psychiatric nurse practitioners, psychologists, and social workers. Insurance carriers often have a hierarchy for payment, with physicians (i.e., psychiatrists) at the top and master's level non-medical providers (i.e., counselors and social workers) at the bottom. Using the example above, it may be that psychiatrists are reimbursed by insurers at $140 for that service while social workers are reimbursed closer to $85. Similarly, psychiatric nurse practitioners who do not accept insurance may charge $200 per therapy session while counselors in the area typically charge $135. In this example, most medical providers do not provide 60 minutes of psychotherapy alone because they tend to prescribe medication. Knowing that, I might charge somewhere near $175 per therapy session for clients, with the expectation that I would likely receive less for a session should I get empaneled with insurance carriers in my region.

The most coveted source of fair market value data for therapists who want to accept insurance is their actual schedule of reimbursement rates for each procedure. However, most carriers require that therapists in their network keep these rates confidential. Sharing such data may constitute a breach of contract, which is why the available public databases are the best option for your research.

METHOD 2: INCOME NEEDS

The second method of determining your fees is based on the financial needs of the individual provider rather than what the market suggests sessions would cost. In essence, therapists first determine what income would allow them to enjoy a comfortable financial life and then work backwards to figure out what to charge to achieve that.

For example, let's say that I determined that the take-home pay (after business expenses and taxes) necessary for me to maintain my lifestyle is $90,000. Let's also suppose that I am comfortable seeing 26 clients weekly and having four weeks off per year. I would need to complete the following calculations to determine my fees for client sessions:

$90,000 / 48 weeks = $1875 weekly net income
$1875 / 26 sessions = $72.12 net per session

To determine the *gross* income required to net that amount per session, I would then factor in expenses of about 35% plus about 10% for taxes:

$72.12 = 100%x - 35%x - 10%
$72.12 = 55%x or .55x
$72.12 / .55 = x
$131.13 = x

Using this method, my average session cost should be about $131 to ensure that my work would provide me a comfortable living. The potential disadvantage of the second method is that the market may not actually bear the fee that I wish to charge. For example, I may realize that insurance company reimbursement for my services as a master's level empaneled provider is only $103. Thus, I would need to possibly see more clients than I'd initially intended or try to cultivate a mix of insurance and private pay clients to achieve an average of $131 per session.

There may be other ways to set your fees, but I recommend using a data-driven approach. Doing a little research at the beginning of your process will help you plan realistically to prevent having unattainable ideas of how much you can expect to receive for your services.

WHAT HAPPENS IF I DECIDE TO TAKE INSURANCE?

As previously discussed, deciding whether to take insurance is an important decision that you should weigh carefully. If you decide to, there are a few steps in the process. Generally speaking, the process is lengthy, lasting anywhere between three and 12 months from start to finish. (Full disclosure: I've done my own credentialing once when I first started my practice.) Dealing with insurance paperwork is often confusing and daunting, even for the most diligent therapist. For this reason, I recommend that therapists either pay for a credentialing service or enlist the help of a mentor and fellow practice owner who has completed the process before. The cost to hire a biller or service is generally around $150-$200 per insurance panel.

If you are working at an existing agency, you will likely be credentialed already with some of the insurers you hope to take. In that case, you may be able to ask questions of the agency's credentialing specialist or simply contact the insurance company to figure out how to add another location to your profile.

Should you decide to undertake the credentialing process alone, here's an overview of the steps:

1. Gather all your professional data, including resume, transcripts, proof of licensure, liability insurance, and NPI
2. Complete or update your CAQH
3. Contact the Provider Relationship department at the desired insurer(s)
4. Complete and submit the insurance company application
5. Wait...most likely for a long time

To restate, I strongly believe it's better to hire a professional to assist you with the credentialing process than to do it yourself. As a novice, you will not likely have the insider information that a biller or credentialing specialist would have, and it will assuredly take you more time than it would take them.

Once you are credentialed, you will sign a contract that says you'll play by the insurance company's rules. Part of signing that contract means that you will accept the rates the insurance company offers you, regardless of the sticker price of your sessions. To return to an example from the previous chapter, if you decide that your fee for CPT code 90837 is $144 but the insurance company will only pay $125.52, you are agreeing that you cannot and will not bill an insured person for the $18.48 difference. To do so is called "balance billing" and is illegal in most states.

"Medical necessity" will likely be another clause in the contract with the insurance company. Essentially this means that you agree only to charge insurance companies for medically necessary services. You also take care to continually assess and document the medical necessity of the care you provide. Conducting formal or informal assessments of treatment progress and client functioning is part of establishing medical necessity. In practice, this means that you can't see a client in perpetuity if their presenting concerns do not warrant doing so.

From a financial point, accepting insurance will greatly expand your pool of potential clients. The tradeoff is that you will most likely be paid less than your advertised fee for particular services, and some services may not be reimbursed at all. Many therapists determine that the sheer volume of clients they see can offset the lower rate paid for those sessions.

Once you're fully empaneled, you'll need to submit insurance claims. Though you can submit the CMS 1500 form for each claim, you'll probably wish to submit all your billing electronically.

If it sounds like the process of dealing with insurance companies can be a pain, that's because it is! Insurance is a multibillion-dollar industry in the U.S., so the systems that govern and manage it are cumbersome and highly regulated. Unless you enjoy the cat-and-mouse game of dealing with insurance companies, I recommend that you outsource most of the insurance-related tasks to maintain your sanity

HOW MUCH SHOULD I SPEND ON RENTING AN OFFICE?

Your therapy office will be a place where your clients laugh, weep, speak their unspeakable secrets, and try to find healing. It is literally the holding environment and container for their pain and distress. Because of its centrality to your work, you should be deliberate about choosing your space. You'll want to ensure that both you and your clients will feel comfortable and as relaxed as possible before signing a rental agreement.

HOW DO I CHOOSE MY OFFICE?

Below are a few questions to consider as you embark upon finding the perfect space for your practice.

- *Do I need my own space, or can I sublet?* If you are planning to establish a full-time practice, it may be more comfortable to have your own office. You may be able to sublet a private office in someone else's suite, which would likely involve less risk. However, you would need to ensure that doing so would be effective and safe for your clients. For example, it would be imprudent for a child-focused practice to sublet space in a suite of forensic psychologists.

- ***Whom do you intend to see, and what are the unique needs of this population?*** If you intend to work as a play therapist with children, your office needs will vastly differ from that of a colleague who works primarily with gender-expansive adults or one who specializes in working with neurodiversity or with couples in crisis. Each of these client demographics would require different office locations and configurations. Whether a space is ADA-compliant, has gender-neutral restrooms, or has waiting rooms with minimal noise can potentially limit what clients you can see.

- ***What is my desired geographic area and why? Is that area convenient for my ideal client?*** Things like the convenient parking or highway accessibility are important for clients who drive, just as proximity to public transportation may be to those clients who don't. Similarly, just because *you* may feel comfortable in a wealthy, suburban neighborhood doesn't mean clients with a history of traumatic experience with police will.

- ***Does the space allow me to maintain my ethical and legal obligations?*** A retail space with a large, street-facing window would make maintaining client privacy challenging. Similarly, ensuring that your office allows for PHI to be kept behind double locks is essential to maintaining HIPAA compliance.

Investing time at the beginning of your search to consider these questions will help you avoid making a potentially costly and lengthy mistake in your office selection.

HOW MUCH SPACE DO I NEED?

A big question, and perhaps the first question, to ask yourself is "How much space do I need?" Generally speaking, a nice-sized office is somewhere in the 150-225 square foot space, and a roomy waiting room should be about 200-300 square feet. For a solo practice, 300-400 square feet will create a comfortable office and waiting room that are neither cramped nor cavernous.

HOW MUCH SHOULD I SPEND?

Your budget for office space has a direct impact on your bottom line. A good rule of thumb is to spend no more than 10% of your anticipated income on a space. Even if you're subletting or sharing an office, this calculation will help you keep your practice financially solvent. I'll use an example from my own rental history to illustrate:

When I first expanded from a solo to a group practice, I shared a four-office suite with a colleague. I rented two offices for $700 per month. I hired a graduate student to see clients in one of the offices, and the other was mine. Following my own advice, my calculations for the office suggest our practice must gross at least $3500 per month, per office, to be financially viable:

$700 / 2 offices = $350 per office
$350 = 10% of X
$3500 = X

At the time, my practice averaged about $130 per session. I saw about between 7-8 people weekly, as did my supervisee.

7.5 x $130 = $975 per week,
or about $3900 per month
$3900 / $700 = 5.57%

Since each of us averaged 28-32 clients monthly, our space was affordable even though we both saw clients only part time. Before leasing or subleasing an office space, you can do a similar calculation to avoid paying too much in rent. In some areas of the country where the rents are higher, 10% of your planned income may not enable you to find a space that's comfortable. If that's the case in your area, remember that the less you spend on rent, the fewer sessions you'll have to facilitate to generate a comfortable income.

HOW MUCH SHOULD I SPEND TO FURNISH MY OFFICE?

The methodical way in which I evaluated how much I should spend on rent might lead you to think that I would have been equally prudent when it came to decorating those two offices. Nope. I made mistakes on both ends of the spending spectrum that I'll share with you as a cautionary tale.

But first, here's a fun fact: I LOVE buying furniture. I don't know why, but I've always had a thing for high-end furniture. So, when it came to my personal office, I spared no expense. By the time I leased my first space, I'd just spent two years subletting an office with attractive but poor-quality furniture. In the ten years before that, I had not remotely liked any of the furniture in my offices. Hopefully this context helps you understand how and why I spent $1900 on a sumptuous, custom leather recliner where I would sit, plus another $1200 on the custom sofa for my clients in my new office. My desk and end tables cost about $1000. The final tally revealed that I'd spent about $5000 furnishing one therapy office.

At some point I realized my mistake, so I tried to make up for it by scrimping on the office my supervisee would use. Into the second office I moved a spare sofa and a comfortable but somewhat scuffed leather recliner that didn't quite fit the decor of my new home. The chair reminded me of a vintage library, so I leaned into that design motif and bought a 1930s mahogany secretary desk and some accessories from Target to tie it all together. I probably spent $500 on end tables, lamps, accessories, and artwork to complete the look.

So, how'd it all work out?!? The results were mixed. I loved that my clients felt comfortable in my office, but I'd be distracted when they set their mocha-choca-latte-ya-yas on my end tables without using a coaster. I seethed when their dirty shoes brushed against the sofa that I'd so lovingly selected. I'd get really tense when a client would mistakenly start walking towards my teal leather chair, as if I'd allow their butts to sit there. I'd created an office that I didn't want to share with anyone else, including my clients. Clients (and I) had the opposite reaction to my supervisee's office. I'd be embarrassed when people asked "Did someone give you that?" about the secretary desk with its imperfections that I thought added character. It looked *aiiight*, but the office was more old living room than retro chic library-office.

If it's not yet obvious, there are a few takeaways from my cautionary tale:

1. Set a reasonable budget for each office and stick to it. About $1200 to $1800 per office is a reasonable investment. Discount furniture stores will likely be your friends. My default stores are Home Goods and Home Sense, where you can often find high-quality and/or brand-name items at a great discount. I don't prefer a modern aesthetic, so IKEA doesn't work for me. When the practice moved to a bigger office, I was easily able to furnish each of the four new offices for about $1500 each. Places like Cost Plus World Market

are also good—if you catch a sale. Some people also have luck at stores like Ashley Furniture or Value City Furniture, but I don't tend to like the quality-for-the-price equation for their inventory. Stores like Room and Board, Create and Barrel, Arhaus, Pottery Barn, or West Elm will likely be too expensive to stay within this budget, but miracles can happen.

2. Save on the sofa. You want to find something that's comfortable but ultimately disposable. Your clients are going to plop down, sometimes in wet and/or dirty clothes, snot-cry, and fart there. It's not something in which you should invest heavily. About $500 should be sufficient.

3. Invest in a good therapy chair. I don't recommend spending nearly $2000 like I did, but I will advise that it should be your one splurge item. Your clients are going to sit for less than an hour at a time, but you may be sitting 6-8 hours a day. You don't want that time to be uncomfortable. Find a chair that supports your head, neck, and back and that won't show wear easily. Invest time and reasonable money finding a chair that fits your body well. Between $400 and $500 is about as much as you should pay. Warehouse clubs such as Costco and Sam's Club often have comfortable accent chairs and recliners that fit the bill for as low as $300.

4. Buy neutral colors but avoid anything too light. Ecru will show more dirt and wear than khaki.

5. Accessories and color are really important. Because you'll need more than you think you will, try to grab this stuff cheap at places like HomeGoods and the like.

6. Frame your diplomas and licenses and hang them. I once read that 4-7 framed credentials convey competence without seeming braggadocious. You want people to trust in your competence but not be intimidated by your accomplishments.

Clients are most comfortable in an office that is homey but cleaner than most of their actual homes. You want the furnishings to look middle-of-the-road. Mid-century modern furniture remains stylish, though your office should reflect your personal design sensibility. I'm a transitional design guy, myself. Whether you prefer the creativity of separate pieces chosen to coordinate or the ease of matchy-matchy living room sets, you'll want all the furniture to look like it belongs together. Save the good stuff for your house.

At a minimum, you'll need a place for clients to sit (generally a sofa, though not necessarily), a comfortable chair for yourself, a desk with drawers, a desk chair, tables beside where you and the client will sit, and a locked filing cabinet for any client materials you collect. Whether you do play therapy with kids, couples or family therapy, psychological testing, or any other treatment modality will dictate the type of furniture and accessories that you choose. Textures and materials matter. Buying an off-white velour sofa for the waiting room of your practice specializing in school-aged kids, for example, is not advisable.

Clients are put at ease by warm, natural materials, such as wood, and may be put off by colder finishes like metal, glass, or even leather. Fish tanks, bubbling fountains, and other water features can be soothing, as can plants. Abstract art in muted colors or pictures of nature can help create a healing ambiance in your space. White noise machines are also helpful in masking sounds and ensuring privacy. Function is more important than opulence in your office.

Before the COVID-19 pandemic put a stranglehold on the world, I would have advised new practice owners to consider purchasing hospitality supplies including a water cooler and a single-serve coffee/tea maker with a selection of tea bags, pods, creamers, and sweeteners for your waiting room. I would have also suggested that current magazines reflecting your clients' needs and interests be available. At the time I'm writing this, however, I would advise against placing anything in your office that cannot be sanitized. In my own waiting room, we have exchanged the large three-seat, cloth-covered sofa for vinyl-coated individual chairs that can be easily wiped down and separated. Practice owners at this moment are trying to navigate what waiting rooms will look like post-pandemic, so we can't yet know how to best plan for client comfort. Other amenities such as soft music (e.g., smooth jazz, instrumental R&B, classical) can help to create a soothing atmosphere without the potential for spreading disease.

HOW DO I SELECT A HEALTH RECORDS SYSTEM?

As your training has taught you, documenting clinical material is a legal and ethical mandate. What you document may vary based on the ethics of your discipline and the laws of your jurisdiction, but you must maintain adequate records. Therefore, you'll need to spend some time researching your best options for maintaining documentation.

EMRS/EHRS

Electronic medical records (EMRs) or electronic health records (EHRs) are the industry standard at this point. More than a dozen currently on the market are geared specifically toward therapists, and they each have their relative strengths and drawbacks. It is essential to have a user-friendly portal that allows clients to access and update forms, request appointments, and pay their bills. You also want to ensure the kind of functionality your specific practice requires. For example, you may want to easily upload or import a photo of a drawing that your art therapy client created or a genogram that you worked on with your couple. The COVID-19 pandemic demonstrated the importance of having an integrated telehealth platform within your EHR as well. Finally, for insurance-based practices, the ability to generate and submit insurance claims, verify benefits, and create client Super Bills through the EHR will be essential. Simple Practice and Therapy Notes are two of the most popular, but you can easily find reviews of EHRs online as you research. Most also provide a free trial period to allow you to test their functionality. Again, they all do pretty much the same thing, so pick the one you like best and move on.

HOW DO I MANAGE THE FINANCES IN A PRIVATE PRACTICE?

Therapists are sometimes good with feelings but bad with money. I'll try to help you avoid that trap. The big issue that therapists have is commingling their money. Whether they don't separate their business income from their personal accounts, or they fail to account for quarterly taxes and other expenses, the major problem is that therapists don't keep money separate which makes accounting for big and small expenses challenging. Parsing the money into different accounts allows you to keep better track of spending. Failing to do so ultimately does many practice owners in.

Earlier, I recommended that you open at least three business banking accounts. I'll explain why now.

1. Your first account needs to be for money received. This will be the account into which your direct deposits from insurance payers, credit payments, checks, cash, and other payment for your therapy services will flow.

2. The second account is for your quarterly taxes; into this account you'll transfer 5-10% of everything that comes into your first account. This should be a checking account from which you pay your quarterly taxes. If you have excess money in this account after pay your personal taxes in April, you can transfer it to your personal account as a reward for effective financial planning!
3. The third account is for your expenses. This is another checking account that you'll use to pay for everything else: office rent, Internet and phone, utilities, continuing education, license renewal, equipment, software, insurance, and other stuff to help the business function. You should transfer into this account 30-35% of everything that comes into your first account. By ensuring your expenses never exceed this account's balance, you will avoid overspending.
4. You will also use an existing personal account for what you pay yourself. You will transfer 55-60% of what you receive on your self-assigned payday.

I recommend transferring money from the first account to the others on the first day of each month, though you may choose to do so more frequently if you want to pay yourself more often. The percentages listed above are conservative. Unless you're in a high-rent area or repeat my mistakes in furnishing your office, it's likely that your expenses will be far less than 35% of your total income. At the end of the year, you can transfer any unspent money in your expense account to your personal account. Or, you may choose to let any excess funds accumulate to start saving for future expenses.

I find this system useful to help me keep track of my expenses and save enough money for my quarterly taxes. Separating my taxes and expenses from my take-home pay allows me to avoid spending what looks like "extra money" and to avoid scrambling when tax time comes. Using an envelope system like this is simple. Moreover, it helps you quickly know if you have a money leak in your business. If you're continually close to the minimum balance in your Expenses account, then you can see that you're overspending in some way, set about figuring out how and why, and then fix it.

I won't bore you with tips on using QuickBooks or other accounting software. I will, however, encourage you to get an accountant. If you're anything like me, you'd rather not spend your time tracking expenses in a spreadsheet. It's tedious and generally not a good use of your time. Accounting and bookkeeping help can range from about $100 to nearly $1000 monthly, depending on the services provided. If you insist on doing it yourself, there are also training programs specifically targeted to therapists to learn how to effectively manage your money. These online classes usually cost around $500 and can easily be found with a quick internet search.

HOW DO I EFFECTIVELY MARKET THE PRACTICE?

Marketing is perhaps the most important business function of the private practice. As in any business, sales are the foundation of your practice. Remember that the purpose of your practice is to be profitable. In the case of private practices, sales translate into having a sufficient and consistent client flow to generate enough income to be profitable.

The amount and types of marketing you'll need to employ will depend first on whether you intend to accept insurance. One important benefit of getting empaneled with insurance carriers is the steady stream of client referrals you receive. Insurance companies publish online directories and many have care navigators to help their members find appropriate treatment. Depending on the panels you're on, you may not need to do any additional marketing to get and maintain a full caseload. That being said, you will likely want to engage the services of a therapist directory to supplement insurance directory listings or replace them if you don't take insurance.

THERAPIST DIRECTORIES

For a long time, the Therapist Directory on *Psychology Today* (PT) was the only game in town. It's still the biggest general listing for therapists. At the time I'm writing this, PT gives new subscribers six months of free listing services, which makes it a relatively low-risk advertising avenue. Other general directories like GoodTherapy.com and TherapyDen.com have emerged in recent years; and, while they aren't as exhaustive or well-utilized as PT, many therapists find them helpful in securing leads. Specialized directories focusing on particular clinical issues or client demographics may supplement or even eliminate the need for using a general directory. Dr. Joy Harden Bradford's TherapyforBlack-Girls.com is a brilliant resource that effectively reaches thousands of Black women across the country and even the world. Other directories for sexual and gender minorities, couples therapy, sex therapy, and myriad other presenting concerns exist, though their traffic may not justify the cost of subscribing. In either case, many clients find their therapists through a simple internet search, so having a page on a directory, in addition to a webpage, will greatly increase your chances of being found.

WEBSITES

As I mentioned above, you need some sort of web presence. Even if you get a steady stream of client referrals from insurance panels, clients are likely to look you up to verify that you're someone they think they want see. Your website is the most effective and controlled way of providing that information. You can use platforms like Wix.com to create websites yourself relatively easily, and there are specialty website builders like BrighterVision.com or TherapySites.com that focus on meeting the needs of psychotherapists. If you're more technically inclined, you can create your own WordPress site. There are technical experts who help with search engine optimization (SEO) keywords, and other things to get and keep you at the top of search results. There are other tricks like having a blog or vlog that lives on your page that can boost your SEO, thereby increasing the likelihood of generating leads, that you can try too. At minimum, you just need a clean, updated, and professional-looking web presence.

SOCIAL MEDIA

Lots of therapists create Facebook pages, Instagram accounts, TikTok videos, and all manner of social media to advertise their practices with varying degrees of success. Inspirational quotes, videos, and the like may eventually go viral and produce viable client leads... or they may be drowned out by louder voices of wellness influencers who are free from the ethical and legal mandates of licensure and who can post whatever they choose. In my experience, social media can help promote your practice or build name recognition but it's not the most efficient strategy for building a full caseload. Nevertheless, it does work for lots of people. You may want to try and see if it works for you.

NETWORKING

The endgame for networking is to increase the likelihood that other people will refer clients to you. Depending on the type of practice you're building, you may wish to use direct or indirect strategies, or both, to connect with potential referral partners in your community. Indirect strategies might include giving presentations about your specialty area to a professional or community audience. Contacting the administration at a private school to offer to talk to students and/or school staff about managing stress related to high stakes testing might yield referrals if your practice specializes in anxiety disorders among teens. You may also give a more basic talk about stress management to the local chamber of commerce. The goal of indirect strategies is to establish your reputation as an expert to whom folks in the community can refer. Giving away your time and expertise is likely to curry favor among potential referees, which can help you stand out.

When using direct strategies, the idea is to directly solicit referrals from one source or another. For example, if your expertise is in perinatal mental health, you may decide to contact all the midwife practices within two miles of your office to let them know about your openings. You could also contact other clinicians specializing in perinatal mental health in your area and ask them to refer to you those clients they don't have the capacity to see. Direct strategies are an appeal to potential partners who have easy access to your ideal client.

Your ability to attract and retain the clients is essential to having a thriving business. Because of the dearth of mental health providers in this country, you will not likely have to employ more than a few strategies to fill your practice. It can sometimes feel smarmy to think of selling your services to the general public, as most of us come to see our work as a calling. Nonetheless, you must face the facts that we are *selling* our services, so we need to market them. Black therapists make up a disproportionate minority of clinicians, which will likely work in your favor. Nonetheless, it would be a mistake to assume that being on insurance panels or word-of-mouth alone will generate enough leads to create a viable practice.

WHAT KIND OF SUPPORT WILL I NEED?

When you first start your practice, you'll probably have to do everything from answering the phone and responding to messages to taking the trash out of your office to arguing with insurance companies about claims denials. As your caseload fills and money flows into the practice, you'll be able to identify the things that you prefer handling on your own and then farm out the rest. Below I've identified some of the most common tasks that practice owners outsource, as well as the clinical support they may engage to ensure their practices are functioning optimally.

FRONT-LINE CLIENT CONTACT

There's some research that suggests that for every day that a potential therapy client waits for a response from you—their potential therapist—the likelihood of them engaging in therapy decreases 18-25%. As a private practice therapist, you'll spend most of your work time providing therapy, so you won't be readily available to answer every phone call or respond to each email in a timely manner. To lower the anxiety of having to get back to each client, you may want to invest in a virtual assistant (VA) to provide some or all of your scheduling contacts with clients. I've seen this sort of support range from a VA spending 15 minutes per day retrieving voicemail for the practice to engaging a VA service to respond to all client emails and phone calls. This is typically one of the first tasks that therapists outsource. From a financial perspective, it's always more cost effective to pay a VA $20 an hour to complete some tasks to avoid foregoing the $45-$200 an hour you would lose by not using that time in session with a client. A good VA will often pay for themself, as they usually help you to schedule more clients than you would be able to do on your own. They may also help with other important tasks like verifying a client's insurance benefits prior to their first appointment, which can significantly decrease the likelihood of conducting sessions that may never be reimbursed.

CLAIMS AND BILLING

In addition to verifying benefits, administrative support can fulfill myriad other duties, which will greatly enhance your efficiency and quality of life. For insurance-based practices, managing the revenue cycle can be daunting. At the simplest level, you can work with a biller who will submit your insurance claims electronically for you; this speeds up the reimbursement process significantly. Billers may charge a percentage of the revenue that they bill and collect, or they may charge an hourly rate. As I mentioned earlier, most EHRs can quickly and efficiently submit claims to insurance companies (or claims clearinghouses), allowing you to submit your own claims. But dealing with insurance companies about claims rejections and mistakes can be a time- and labor-intensive process. Billers can be invaluable to you in navigating these sorts of struggles, as they typically have a wealth of knowledge about how to effectively get claims paid that you, the clinician, do not have. Additionally, full-service billers can also assist in reconciling insurance claims to ensure that they are submitted and paid promptly. Preventing substantial revenue loss can also help offset the cost of hiring a billing specialist for an insurance-based practice.

ACCOUNTING AND BOOKKEEPING

Regardless of if you take an insurance or have a cash-pay practice, you will need to adequately record and categorize your business-related expenses. Hiring a bookkeeper may help you determine which expenses are deductible, monitor your spending, and avoid overspending. Most practice owners start off keeping their own books, but as the business and the expenses grow, doing so can become untenable.

Accountants, specifically tax accountants, are other professionals whom every small business owner should employ. As an entrepreneur, you'll be responsible for paying taxes on a quarterly basis, and a tax accountant can help you plan adequately so that you're not stuck with a whopping tax bill in April. The number one financial mistake new private practitioners make is failing to set aside enough money for taxes. Engaging an accountant or accounting firm is a crucial step in planning for the success of your business. In fact, I recommend finding a good tax accountant before outsourcing anything else! Avoiding tax penalties and audits is worth whatever it costs you.

CLINICAL CONSULTATION AND PEER SUPERVISION

Even for introverts, the work of therapy can be isolating. Your client pours out their deepest fears, hopes, and struggles to you while you must keep their confidence. Working in a solo practice magnifies this dynamic. There won't be anyone in the hallways with whom you can celebrate your wins or talk through your struggles between sessions.

Peer supervision groups can be a wonderful way of creating community while also finding the clinical support that you need. These groups can be focused on a shared theoretical orientation or a book. A collection of friends and strangers who trust each other enough to be vulnerable with challenging cases might provide invaluable social interaction and insight. If groups aren't your thing, you can enlist the services of a clinical consultant or supervisor with whom you can share your challenging cases and ethical dilemmas.

Practicing in isolation substantially increases the risk of unethical, illegal, or just problematic behaviors. In fact, many licensing board sanctions are against clinicians working in solo private practice. It's a smart preventive step to ensure that you have colleagues in whom you can confide and whom you trust to provide feedback on your clinical work.

It can be challenging for practice owners to spend money on things they've been used to doing themselves. Practice coaches have lots of ways to say this such as "staying in your zone of genius" or "maximizing your time by doing only high-dollar activities." I agree with those explanations, but I also see outsourcing as a means of increasing your freedom. You didn't leave the security of a job with steady paycheck with responsibilities that you don't enjoy only to create more unappealing tasks in your own practice. The freedom that most of us seek in entrepreneurship is the ability to do only the things that bring us joy. Once your practice can afford to allot 5-10% of the total income for external support, I strongly recommend that you outsource the more mundane tasks of practice management. I promise, it makes the experience more enjoyable when you're not doing everything alone.

CONCLUSION

I hope that what you read has either emboldened you to pursue your dream of opening a private practice or has elucidated all the reasons why you shouldn't.

There are countless resources available on the internet to help you. Accounting firms, EHR companies, marketing companies, and practice-building coaches offer tipsheets and other tangible supports to help you learn what it takes to open up a business. And over the last five years or so, podcasts focusing on building and growing a private practice have increased in number and quality. There's a world of help available to you if you need it. You're not alone in this. Many, many people want you to succeed—including me.

Whether you decide to start a solo private practice, a group practice, or work for an agency, I hope that your next career step brings you a sense of emotional fulfillment and financial stability. The work you're doing—caring for Black folks—is incredibly necessary. In the face of all the trauma that we have and continue to endure, the comfort that you provide to your clients strengthens them and the community as a whole. I wish you nothing but success. And I thank you wholeheartedly for helping to infuse more positivity into the world.

Take good care,
David Goode-Cross

Dr. David Goode-Cross is a licensed counseling psychologist and the owner of East Towson Psychological Services, a group practice specializing in working with the intersections of BIPOC and LGBTQIA+ identities in the Baltimore area. Prior to starting the practice, Dr. Goode-Cross served on the faculties of West Virginia University and the University of Baltimore as well as working in collegiate mental health in such schools as The Ohio State University, The College of William & Mary, American University, and Maryland Institute College of Art. His scholarship on issues of African American mental health has been published in such peer-reviewed journals as the *Journal of Black Psychology*, *Psychology of Men and Masculinity*, the *Journal of Homosexuality*, and *Training and Education in Professional Psychology*.

www.ingramcontent.com/pod-product-compliance
Lightning Source LLC
Chambersburg PA
CBHW050808160726
48004CB00002B/752